MACHINES AT WORK

Emergency!

IAN GRAHAM

QED Publishing

A Catalogue record for this book is available from the British Library.

ISBN 1 84538 363 X

Written by Ian Graham
Designed by Calcium
Editor Sarah Eason
Foldout illustation by Ian Naylor
Picture Researcher Joanne Forrest Smith

Publisher Steve Evans
Editorial Director Jean Coppendale
Art Director Zeta Davies

Printed and bound in China

Picture credits
Key: t = top, b = bottom, c = centre, l = left, r = right, FC = front cover

Alamy/FC South West Images, Scotland; John Blair 5TC, /don jon red 15TR, /Michael Dwyer 14-15,
/Alan Novelli 12BL, /Chuck Pefley 13CR, /The Photo Library Wales 6-7; **Brentwood Police Dept.**
13TL; **CRASAR**/University of South Florida 29BR; **Corbis** 22, /Robin Adshead/The Military Picture
Library 28-29, /Bruce Chambers 22-23, /Ashley Cooper 4BL, /Rick Friedman 29TL, /George Hall 21TL,
/Peter Turnley 24-25, /PHCN Terry C Mitchell 10-11, /Reuters 23CR, 24BL, 26BL, /Patrick Ward 15CL;
Crown Copyright/MOD/8-9, /Jack Pritchard 9C Images from www.photos.mod.uk Reproduced with
the permission of the Controller of Her Majesty's Stationery Office; **Deep Flight** 33BC; **Freefoto**/
Ian Britton 4-5, 12-13, 21BL; **Genesis**/NASA 30-31, 32-33; **Jaguar Daimler Heritage Trust** 20TR;
NASA 31, 32BL, 33TR; **Nordic Marine** 7BR; **OshKosh Trucks** 26-27, 27TR; **Pierce
Manufacturing** 3, 16, 21; **RNLI**/Tom Collins 7TL; **US Navy**/Dave Fliesen 10BL;
Underwater Contractor International 11TL.

Words in **bold** can be found in the Glossary on page 34.

CONTENTS

EMERGENCY MACHINES

When accidents happen or disaster strikes, emergency machines rush to the rescue with well-trained crews. There are many different types of emergency machines from cars, vans and trucks to motorbikes, helicopters, aeroplanes, boats, ships and even submarines. Most carry special equipment and supplies at all times – there is never time to pack when an emergency call comes!

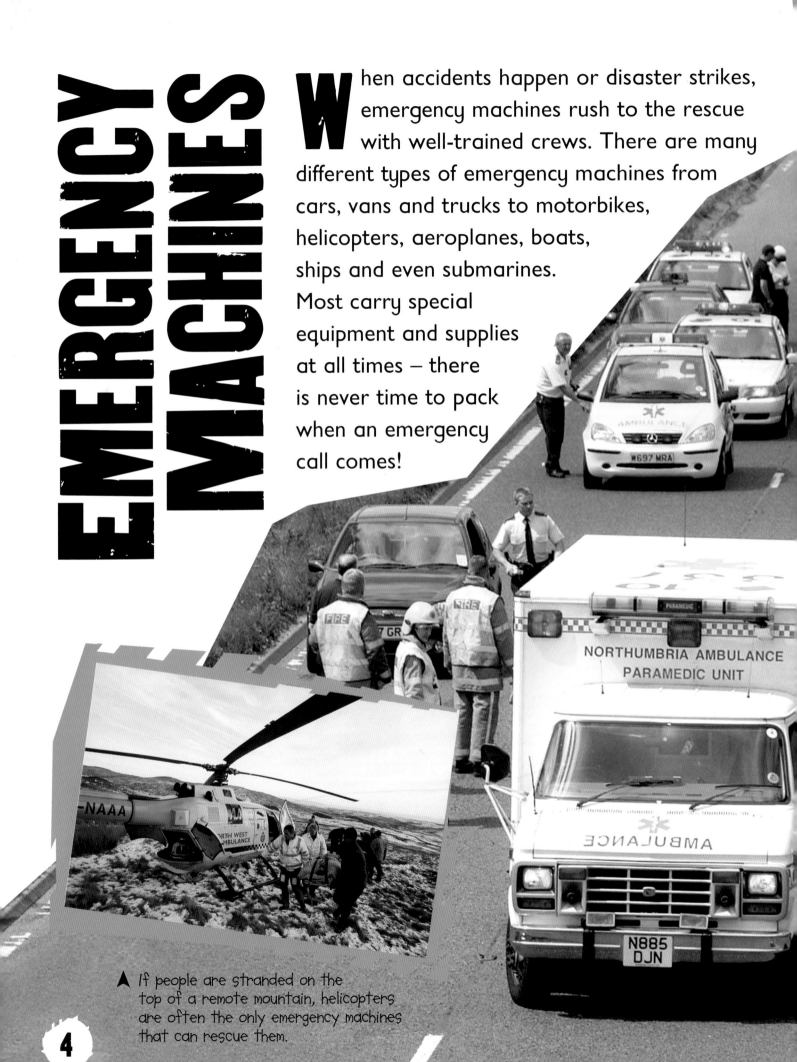

▲ If people are stranded on the top of a remote mountain, helicopters are often the only emergency machines that can rescue them.

MACHINE POWER

Emergency vehicles are stocked with lots of special equipment. Fire engines have pumps that spray large amounts of water over fires. They also carry powerful cutting tools to release people trapped inside cars or buildings. Firefighting aeroplanes have big water tanks that can be emptied over a fire in a matter of seconds.

◀ The lockers inside a fire engine are packed with extra tools, hoses, equipment and supplies.

◀ Different types of emergency vehicles and their crews work together to deal with major accidents and emergencies.

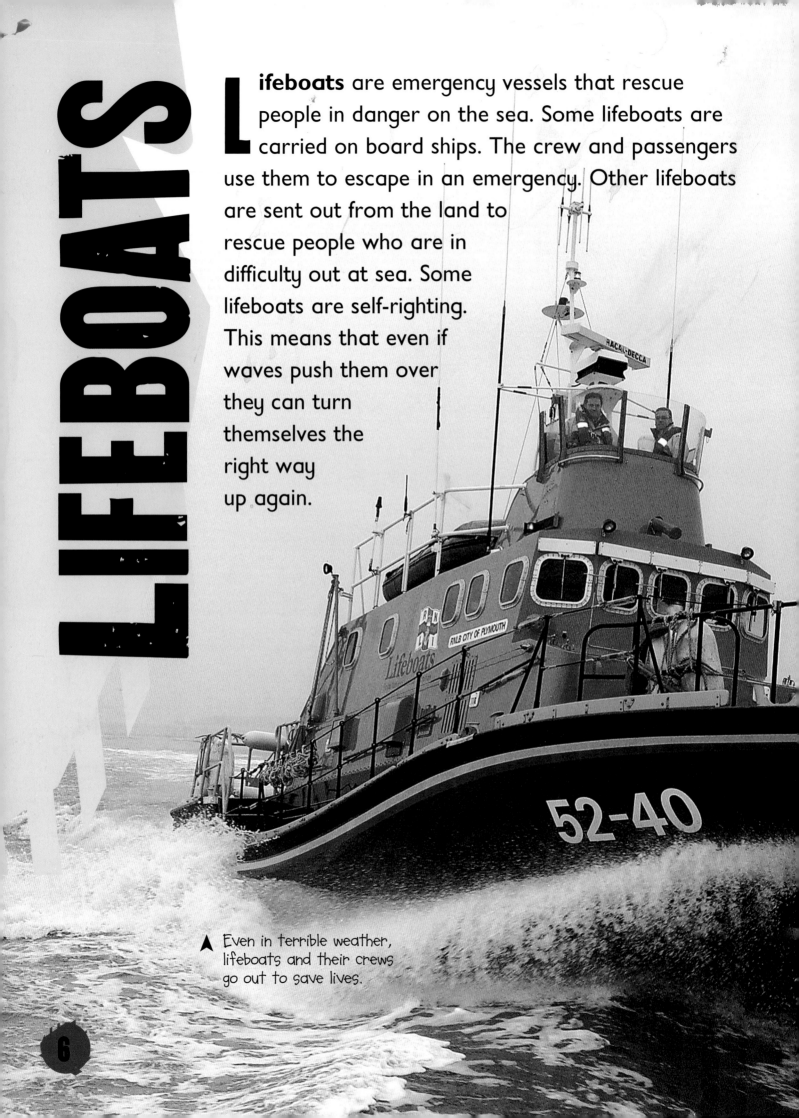

LIFEBOATS

Lifeboats are emergency vessels that rescue people in danger on the sea. Some lifeboats are carried on board ships. The crew and passengers use them to escape in an emergency. Other lifeboats are sent out from the land to rescue people who are in difficulty out at sea. Some lifeboats are self-righting. This means that even if waves push them over they can turn themselves the right way up again.

▲ Even in terrible weather, lifeboats and their crews go out to save lives.

SURF RESCUE

Small inflatable boats rescue people in shallow waters near the shore. These boats have flat bases and are made from a rubber tube filled with air. Rigid Inflatable Boats, also called RIBs, rescue people further from the shore. RIBs have a hard plastic hull with a rubber tube around the top.

◄ Surf rescue boats go to the aid of surfers and swimmers in difficulty.

FACT!

The first lifeboat was designed and built in the 1780s by an Englishman called Lionel Lukin.

Offshore emergency

Giant platforms in the sea drill for oil and gas under the seabed. They have their own lifeboats, which workers use in an emergency. Each of these lifeboats is sealed shut so that it will float in even the roughest of seas!

▲ The survival boats of oil-rig platforms are completely watertight to protect the passengers inside.

AIR RESCUE

The fastest way to find and rescue people in remote places is to use aircraft. Helicopters are ideal for rescue work because they can **hover** over one spot and can land almost anywhere. Aeroplanes cannot hover like helicopters and they need runways to land on. However, they can fly faster than helicopters and can search large areas more quickly. They can also carry out rescue flights over long distances.

▲ Search and rescue helicopters can lift people to safety using a machine called a **winch**.

▼ Sea King helicopters
take part in all
sorts of rescues on
mountains, in remote
countryside and
over the sea.

KING OF THE SEA

The Sea King is one of the most
widely used search and rescue
helicopters. It is a big aircraft with
rotor blades that are nearly 20m
across – that's the length of more
than six cars! It can weigh almost
10 tonnes and carry more than
20 people or nine stretchers
plus doctors.

UNDERWATER EMERGENCIES

Underwater emergency vehicles rescue sailors trapped in sunken submarines. Some of these emergency machines are **submersibles** and others are **diving bells** that are lowered on the end of a long cable. Remotely Operated Vehicles, or **ROVs**, are also used in submarine rescues. An ROV does not have a crew. It is 'driven' by an operator in a nearby ship and has gripping and cutting tools to free a trapped submersible.

▼ The LR5 rescue sub has a crew of three — a pilot, co-pilot and a systems officer.

Rescue sub

The LR5 rescue sub can dive to about 400m and rescue 15 people at a time. It lands on top of the escape hatch of a sunken submarine. The trapped sailors can then climb up to safety through the hatch and into the rescue vehicle.

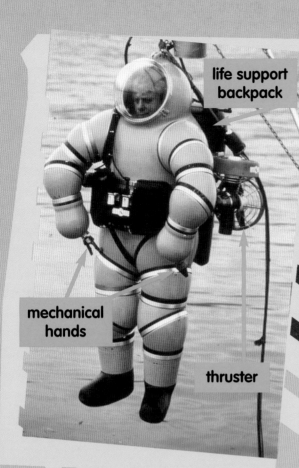

life support backpack

mechanical hands

thruster

HARDSUIT

A strong, rigid metal suit called a hardsuit can withstand the pressure of deep water. Divers wear hardsuits when diving in very deep water. The suit has its own propellers, or thrusters, at the back to move it around through the water. It looks a bit like a space suit!

◄ Divers can wear hardsuits to reach sunken submersibles so that they can help with the rescue operation.

▲ The US Navy's Deep Submergence Rescue Vehicle (DSRV) can dive to a depth of over 1.5km.

POLICE VEHICLES

The police are often the first people to arrive at emergencies of different kinds. Police officers travel in cars packed with computer and radio equipment. Police cars are also called cruisers, squad cars and patrol cars. Most are brightly painted so everyone can see them, but some look like ordinary cars so that officers can travel around without being noticed.

▲ Police cars like this American Ford Crown Victoria are ordinary cars that have been strengthened and improved specially for police work.

◀ Police forces use trained dogs to search for missing people. The dogs are carried in special vans with a cage at the back.

Police technology

Most police cars now have a laptop computer inside. This means officers can check information about people and cars on the main police computer when they are out on the road. Some cars have a video camera and a **radar** system for checking the speed of other vehicles.

◄ Police officers keep in touch with each other by radio. Their cars may also have computer, video and radar equipment to help them catch people who break the law.

Police boats are ➤ used for dealing with emergencies on the water.

AIR FORCE

Police helicopters allow officers to search the ground faster than officers on foot. They can often spot escaping criminals from the air. Their cameras record pictures of events on the ground, such as car chases. At night they can light up the ground with powerful lights or use thermal cameras **that can 'see' in the dark.**

◄ Police helicopters like this Eurocopter EC–135 are used to track criminals in cars or on foot.

AMBULANCES

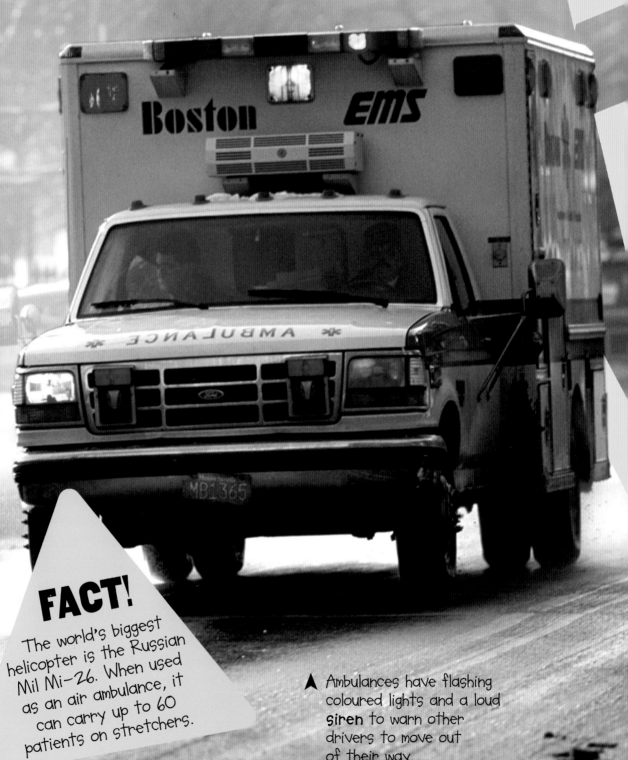

Ambulances are packed with medical equipment. This means that the crew can treat people while they are being taken to hospital. There is room inside for patients who need to lie on stretchers. They are looked after by people called paramedics, who are trained to give emergency medical help.

Boston EMS

AMBULANCE

MB1365

FACT!
The world's biggest helicopter is the Russian Mil Mi-26. When used as an air ambulance, it can carry up to 60 patients on stretchers.

▲ Ambulances have flashing coloured lights and a loud **siren** to warn other drivers to move out of their way.

Air ambulances

Some people are so ill or badly hurt that they have to be moved quickly to hospital by air. An **air ambulance** is a helicopter that can carry patients to hospital much faster than a road ambulance.

Air ambulances have space for ➤ sick or injured people on stretchers. They also carry medical equipment so that the crew can care for patients during their flight.

FLYING DOCTORS

Australia is a huge country and many people live far away from the hospitals in towns and cities. In these places, emergency medical help is provided by the Royal Flying Doctor Service. Every day, its aircraft fly more than 50 000km and its doctors help more than 500 people.

◄ The Royal Flying Doctor Service's aircraft have been helping people in remote parts of Australia since 1928.

The cabin of an air ➤ ambulance aeroplane has beds and lots of medical equipment. It looks like a small hospital.

ladder
can extend to a
height of 30m

rams
lengthen to
raise the ladder

water pipe
carries water up the ladder

high-pressure oil
makes the ram extend
with great force

A fire engine's ladder ➤
has many sections that
slide inside each other.

lockers
contain extra tools
and equipment

FIRE BOATS

Fire boats are firefighting vessels that deal with fires on ships. They suck in seawater and pump it out over the fire. Each boat has several nozzles so that water can be directed onto different parts of a burning ship.

Seawater is pumped out of a fire boat with such force that it can fly more than 100m in the air! ➤

FACT!

The world's most powerful fire boat is the Los Angeles Fire Department's Fireboat number 2. The 32m–long boat can pump almost 145 000 litres of water every minute.

◄ Firefighters going into smoke–filled buildings wear a special mask to keep out smoke and fire. They also breathe air from a tank on their back.

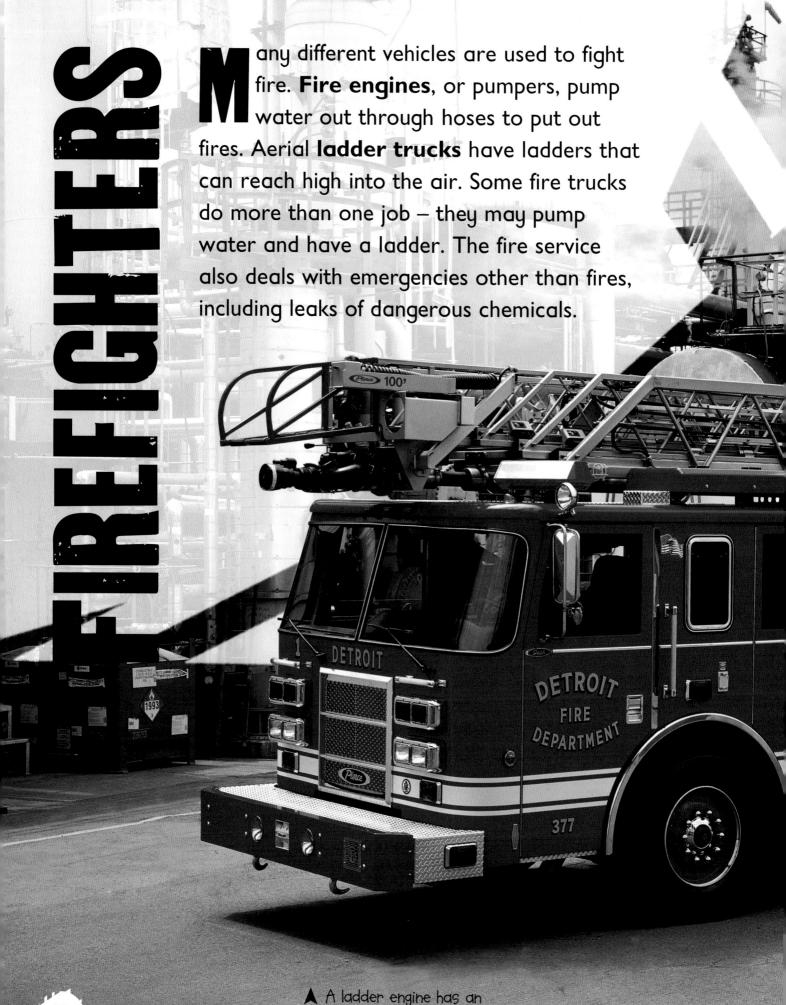

FIREFIGHTERS

Many different vehicles are used to fight fire. **Fire engines**, or pumpers, pump water out through hoses to put out fires. Aerial **ladder trucks** have ladders that can reach high into the air. Some fire trucks do more than one job – they may pump water and have a ladder. The fire service also deals with emergencies other than fires, including leaks of dangerous chemicals.

▲ A ladder engine has an extending ladder on the top.

LADDERS AND PLATFORMS

Ladders and platforms lift firefighters high above the ground. A pipe runs the length of the ladder and carries water to nozzles at the top. As well as fighting fires, ladders and platforms help firefighters to rescue people from tall buildings.

◄ The tallest aerial ladders and platforms can reach more than 30m above the ground.

Jaws of life

As well as putting out fires, firefighters also rescue people trapped in vehicles after road accidents. They use specially designed tools, often called the 'jaws of life'. These can slice through metal and force apart pieces of wreckage.

▲ The 'jaws of life' cutters carried by firefighting vehicles can chop off a car's roof in seconds to reach people trapped inside.

FIRE CHASER

The first car to go faster than the speed of sound was called the Thrust SSC. It was so fast that a specially designed firefighting vehicle was created to reach the car in super-fast time if it caught fire. It was called the Jaguar XLR 'Firechase' car and could reach speeds of 250km/h. Fortunately, it never had to be used.

▼ Jaguar firefighting cars are designed to reach the fastest cars on Earth as quickly as possible.

Heat vision

Smoke makes it difficult for firefighters to see each other inside a burning building. They use special cameras, called **thermal cameras**, to find their way around. Thermal cameras make pictures from heat instead of light and can 'see' in complete darkness. Through a thermal camera hot things, such as flames or someone's body, look bright and cooler things look dark.

◄ This picture of a firefighter was taken by a thermal camera.

Fire engines

Fire engines are built to carry a team of firefighters and all the equipment they need to put out a fire. Water from a tank inside the vehicle is pumped out onto the fire through hoses. If more water is needed, it can be taken from underground water pipes. Hoses, tools and other equipment are carried in cupboards called lockers. Most fire engines are red, but in some places you might also see bright green or yellow fire engines.

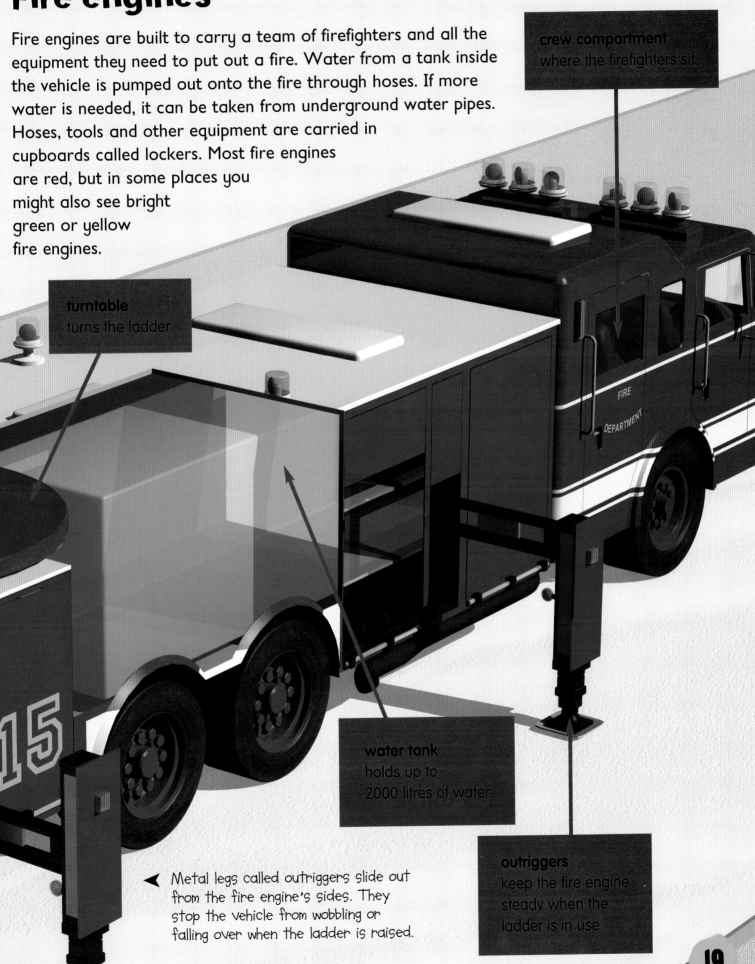

crew compartment
where the firefighters sit

turntable
turns the ladder

water tank
holds up to
2000 litres of water

outriggers
keep the fire engine
steady when the
ladder is in use

◄ Metal legs called outriggers slide out from the fire engine's sides. They stop the vehicle from wobbling or falling over when the ladder is raised.

19

FIREFIGHTING AIRCRAFT

Some fires are so big, or so difficult for firefighters to get to, that they are fought by aircraft. Ordinary aeroplanes and helicopters can be used for this work, but there are also specially designed firefighting aircraft. They fight fires by dropping water, foam or chemicals onto them. The chemicals are often coloured bright red. The colour stains the ground so that pilots can see where the chemicals have landed.

Firehawk

The Sikorsky Firehawk is a firefighting helicopter. To take in water, it hovers just above the surface of the water while a special pipe called a snorkel hose is lowered down to suck up water into the tank.

The Sikorsky ➤ Firehawk helicopter can fill its 3500-litre water tank in only 60 seconds. It then flies off to drop the water onto large fires.

22

◄ A Douglas Invader firefighting plane swoops over a fire and drenches it with chemicals

FLYING BOAT

The Bombardier 415 is specially designed for firefighting. It's a flying boat, so it can land on water as well as fly through the air. It can scoop up more than 6000 litres of water in just 12 seconds before it takes off again. It then flies over the fire and drops the water on it.

▲ Doors in the bottom of the Bombardier 415 open to drop its load of water.

DISASTER HELP

When a flood, **famine** or **hurricane** strikes and large numbers of people need help, huge **cargo** aeroplanes full of supplies fly to their aid. These giant aeroplanes usually move equipment for armies or fly goods from country to country. One of the largest of all cargo aeroplanes is the Lockheed C-5 Galaxy. The whole nose and tail of this aeroplane lift up so that supplies can be loaded onto it. In an emergency, cargo aeroplanes carry life-saving supplies to airports near the disaster. From there, smaller aeroplanes, helicopters and trucks move the supplies to where they are needed.

Helicopter aid

Helicopters are ideal aircraft for delivering emergency supplies. They can land on a small area, or hover close to the ground and hand out boxes of supplies.

◄ Army helicopters deliver emergency supplies after a natural disaster.

Supplies are loaded ➤
onto a Lockheed
C-5 Galaxy on
platforms. Rollers
in the aeroplane's
floor make it
easier to slide
heavy loads
across it.

FACT!
The world's biggest
cargo aeroplane is the
Russian Antonov
An-124. Bigger than
a jumbo jet, it can carry
more than 150 tonnes
of cargo.

AIRPORT FIREFIGHTERS

Every big airport has its own firefighting service which deals with spilled fuel, fires and crashed aircraft. They also help with medical emergenci[es]. Airport firefighting vehicles are called Aircraft Resc[ue] and Fire Fighting (ARFF) vehicles. Airport fire engin[es] are different from other fire engines because they are specially designed for fighting aircraft fires. Big firefighting vehicles have a nozzle on the roof or front bumper that sprays foam over the fire. Firefighters move a **joystick** to steer the nozzle.

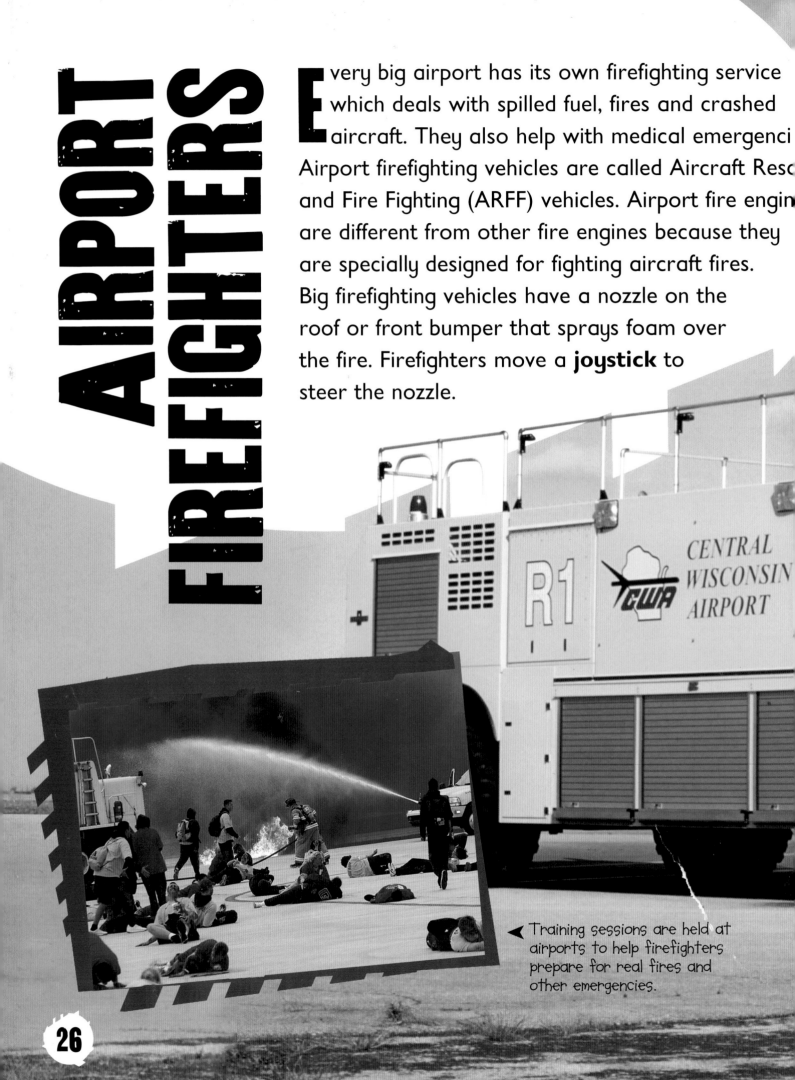

R1 · CENTRAL WISCONSIN AIRPORT

◄ Training sessions are held at airports to help firefighters prepare for real fires and other emergencies.

Reaching inside

Some airport fire engines have a folding mechanical arm on top. A pipe carries water or foam to a nozzle at the end. A firefighter uses a joystick to steer the end of the arm inside the door of a burning aeroplane to soak it with water or foam.

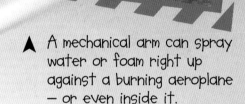

▲ A mechanical arm can spray water or foam right up against a burning aeroplane — or even inside it.

▲ Fires and other emergencies at airports are tackled by a variety of vehicles. These range from small pick-up trucks, carrying medical supplies and tools, to the large firefighting machines.

ROBOTS

Robot rescuers can go into places that are too dangerous for people. They search for survivors in collapsed buildings after an **earthquake** or hurricane, and take water or vital medical help to them. They also help to make unexploded bombs safe. An operator drives the robot. From a safe distance away, the operator sees through the robot's cameras and steers it by moving a small joystick. The robot's mechanical arms can be fitted with a variety of tools to do different jobs.

camera

Like tanks, most ➤ emergency and rescue robots have **tracks** so they can be driven over rough ground.

tracks

dangerous job. The ~~~
sometimes use robots. A robot is driven up to the bomb. The operator can see the bomb from a safe distance through the robot's cameras. The robot's mechanical arm is fitted with tools or a gun to break windows, open doors or pull the bomb out.

◄ Robots carry unexploded bombs away to an area where they can be safely exploded.

gripper camera

gripper

Search and rescue

Search and rescue robots are tiny because they have to be able to get through small spaces in rubble and wreckage. They may look like toys, but they do a very important job.

Search and rescue robots ➤ are used to find people trapped under rubble when buildings collapse. They have lights and cameras to show their operator what they find.

EMERGENCY ROCKETS

Astronauts are launched into space on top of rockets full of explosive fuel. If there is an emergency before take-off, the **astronauts** must be rescued quickly before the rocket fuel explodes. The whole spacecraft can be rescued with the astronauts inside. In fact, the spacecraft itself becomes the rescue vehicle. Russian and Chinese spacecraft have a rocket-powered escape device that flies the spacecraft away to safety.

Emergency rockets ➤
fire and fly
an endangered
spacecraft clear
of the launch pad.

30

SHUTTLE EMERGENCY

If astronauts have to leave a Space Shuttle in a hurry while it is still on the ground, they climb into baskets at the top of the launch tower. The baskets slide down wires to the ground. The astronauts then rush inside an earth-covered room called a bunker, where they will be safe.

Space Shuttle ➤ astronauts practise an emergency escape by sliding more than 600m down a wire in a basket.

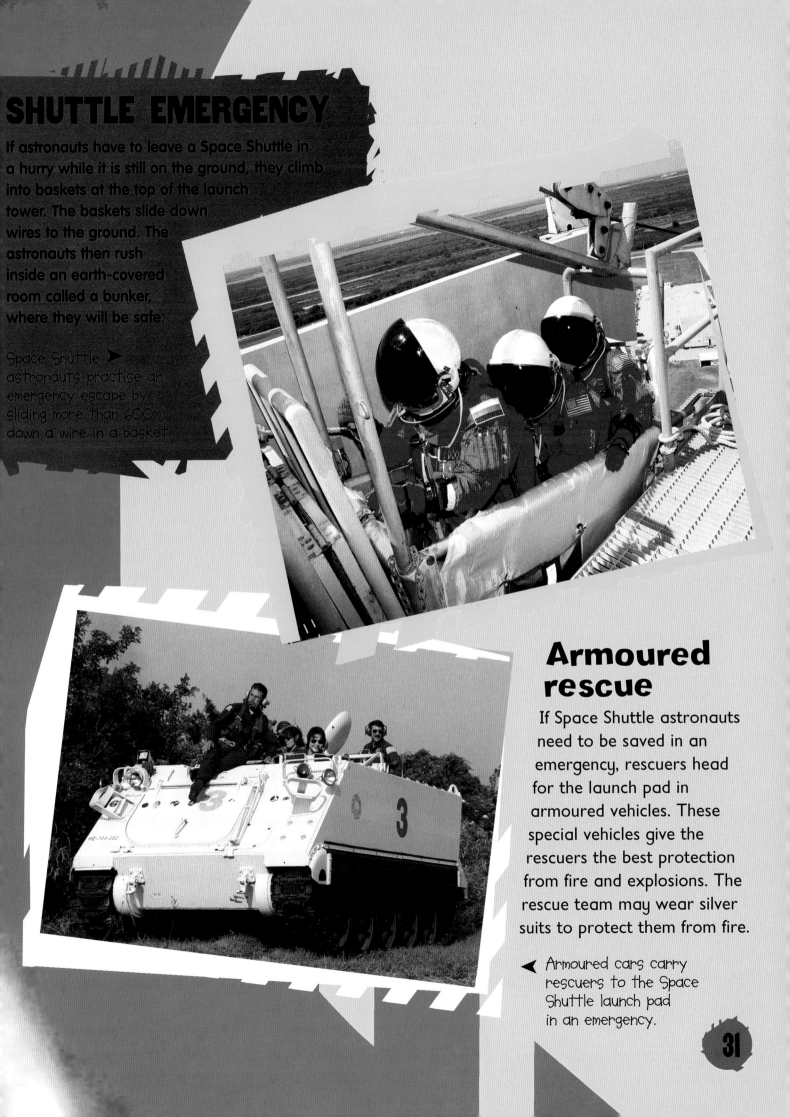

Armoured rescue

If Space Shuttle astronauts need to be saved in an emergency, rescuers head for the launch pad in armoured vehicles. These special vehicles give the rescuers the best protection from fire and explosions. The rescue team may wear silver suits to protect them from fire.

◄ Armoured cars carry rescuers to the Space Shuttle launch pad in an emergency.

31

SPACE RESCUE

Astronauts in space face a variety of dangers. Their spacecraft might catch fire and they might have to leave it in a hurry. An astronaut working outside in space might float away. When a spacecraft is designed, every possible emergency is prepared for, so spacecraft carrying astronauts always have firefighting equipment on board.

A Soyuz spacecraft is always stationed at the ➤ International Space Station, in case the crew has to leave quickly in an emergency.

Safer spacewalks

When astronauts work outside a Space Shuttle or the **International Space Station**, they clip themselves to safety lines which stop them floating away. They also wear a backpack called **SAFER**. If an astronaut does float away, firing jets of gas from SAFER flies the astronaut back to the spacecraft.

◄ The SAFER backpack was first used during the 1995 Space Shuttle Discovery mission.

MOON RESCUE

Some vehicles become emergency rescue machines by accident. The Apollo Lunar Module was designed to land astronauts on the Moon. When part of the Apollo 13 spacecraft exploded on the way to the Moon, the crew used the Lunar Module as a lifeboat to carry them around the Moon and safely back to Earth.

The Apollo Lunar Module saved ➤ the lives of all three of the Apollo 13 crew.

aerial platform   a type of firefighting vehicle with a long arm called a boom that can be raised high into the air. At the end of the boom is a bucket or platform, in which one or two firefighters can stand

air ambulance   an aircraft for carrying sick or injured people

astronaut   someone who travels into space

cargo   goods and materials carried by a ship, aeroplane or lorry

diving bell   a metal tank with an opening at the bottom. Diving bells are lowered into the sea to rescue people trapped in submarines

earthquake   a violent shaking of the ground caused by movements in the Earth's crust

extend   to lengthen and become bigger

famine   a shortage of food in a country, which means that people have very little or nothing to eat

fire engine   a firefighting vehicle that pumps water out through hoses onto a fire. Also called a pumper or pump.

hover   to stay in the same place in the air while flying

hull   the part of a boat or ship that sits in the water

hurricane   a huge circular or spiral-shaped storm with winds powerful enough to flatten some buildings. These violent storms are called hurricanes in the Atlantic Ocean and typhoons in the Indian and Pacific Oceans

inflatable   something that can be filled with air. An inflatable boat has a rubber tube around the top that is filled with air. This helps the boat to float

International Space Station   a huge manned spacecraft that orbits the Earth. Astronauts can live in the space station for several months or even years

joystick   a handle found in a vehicle which can control the movements of the vehicle or its equipment

ladder truck   a firefighting vehicle that has a ladder

lifeboat   a boat specially built for rescuing people at sea

nozzle   a narrow metal tube through which fire engines and fire boats pump water onto fires. A nozzle may be fixed to the vehicle or it may be attached to the end of a hose

radar   a system that uses radio waves to show where ships or planes are

ROV   Remotely Operated Vehicle – a machine controlled from a safe distance by an operator. ROVs are used for dangerous jobs such as making bombs safe

SAFER backpack   a backpack worn by Space Shuttle and International Space Station astronauts when they work outside their spacecraft. If an astronaut drifts away from the spacecraft, he or she can fire jets of gas from the backpack to fly back to safety

siren a piece of equipment that sends out a loud wailing noise

submersible a small craft that can dive into deep water for short periods of time

supersonic faster than the speed of sound

thermal camera a camera that makes pictures from heat instead of light. Also called an infra-red camera or a thermal imaging system

track a belt made from metal sections linked together. Tracked vehicles, like tanks, have a track on each side around their wheels.

vessel a machine that travels on water

winch a machine used to lift or pull heavy objects

FIND OUT MORE

Websites

Discover more about the Royal National Lifeboat Institute and its life-saving boats:
http://www.rnli.org.uk/young.asp

Follow the adventures of Benson the police helicopter:
http://www.thamesvalley.police.uk/news_info/departments/casu/benson1.htm

Find out about lots of different firefighting vehicles from the Florida State Fire College:
http://www.fldfs.com/sfm/bfst/fsfckids/html/fireng.htm

Read about the work of the Australian Surf Life Saving Association:
http://slsa.asn.au

INDEX